How to Become a Funeral Celebrant

The ultimate guide to a successful career

JOHN P FORD

ISBN-13: 978-1499171150

ISBN-10: 1499171153

1st Edition April 2014

Contents

Preface

I have avoided padding out this book with large amounts of copy just to make the reader feel they are getting value for money. I have seen a book on how to become a rail guard that stretched to over 100 pages. I was very impressed with how anyone could manage that, although I suspect that most people would never want to set foot on the train again, much less spend all their working lives after ploughing through that.

Anyone who has attended a training course can recount stories of two days of content that was stretched to five so the training company could justify a larger fee. Topics covered at a snail's pace and lots of 'group discussions' and recaps.

This book contains some of the most potential life changing words you may ever read. Each one will increase your knowledge of the role, how to carry it out, how to be successful. And how to maintain that success.

It would take you less than 10 minutes of your first booking to recoup the cost.

Introduction

The fact that you are reading this suggests you are interested in changing your lifestyle. Perhaps you are planning on retiring soon, or already have and are searching for an extra source of income. You may be in a job that is threatened with redundancy or have already been deemed surplus to requirements. Perhaps you are in a steady career but have had enough of the grinding journey to work followed by countless rounds of meetings, e-mails, performance reviews and all those other seemingly pointless diversions. Tired of having to pretend you are interested in some new initiative handed down from above that looks just like the one you saw five years ago and five years before that. The only difference is the manager keeps getting younger each time. You may feel that you are not actually achieving anything for all the commitment, effort and stress. You may be self-employed but have a requirement or desire to diversify or add another revenue stream.

The internet is full of get rich quick scams and too good to be true schemes for making a fortune from an hours work a day. There are people making lots of money from these, but it's rarely those at the bottom of the food chain, i.e. the likes of you and me. Any person who believes these are a sound investment of their time, energy and money should probably stop reading this now and go down to the bookies.

Apart from winning the lottery, the only way to make money is to work for it. However, there are some ways that are more effective than others. Anyone can stack shelves in a supermarket, and there is nothing wrong with that. Except it pays minimum wage, often involves weekend working and unsociable hours.

The difference between the have and have not's in this world is often the ability to spot an opportunity, weigh up the risks and benefits and then act decisively when the numbers add up. Of course, that's a gross simplification. There are millions of people who, through no fault of their own, find it difficult to make ends meet and improve their lives and those of their families. This can be through the lottery of where and when they were born or the circumstances of their upbringing. Most of us would like to live in a world where we all had the same opportunities and help to make a better life for our families. I doubt anyone who reaches the end of this book, decides to take further action and is successful will disagree with that. However we cannot change the world by ourselves, so all we can do is to look after our own and do what we can, when we can, to help others.

So how have I arrived at this point in my life? Before I describe the opportunity that could change your life, it is worthwhile for you to understand my journey.

Author's Background

During my career, I have re-invented myself several times and learned many lessons about working for others, running a business and how and why people make decisions. I started as an apprentice telecommunications engineer and then moved into sales of technical equipment in the printing industry for 11 years. I then spent a few months as a financial advisor before starting a company with my wife also in the graphics and printing market. This business lasted for ten years and at its peak, gainfully employed seven people. I sold this company when market conditions changed (the risk/reward balance had shifted too far) and went back into the world of employment, in the same market.

It took three attempts over a twelve month period to find an employer who had the right blend of size, opportunity and culture. It's not easy to go back to work for someone after being your own boss for ten years. I knew I was the type of person who wouldn't look back and lament for the business I had created. Yes, it was my baby, but I was not going to let the bank take away my house and make myself unemployable in my industry by leaving my debtors unpaid? Pragmatism is a useful attribute to have in life as it enables you to see the difference between dreams and reality.

During the next ten years, I struggled to find a path on which I was truly happy. I was a good and very successful salesperson in the 1980's and 90's. However as the new century began, I saw a change in attitudes. People were becoming more cynical, less willing to make decisions, more risk averse. In the print industry, many manufacturers appointed dealers to help sell their products. Increasingly they were willing to take actions that undermined that relationship for short-term gain. Customers began to realise that they could play one off against the other to gain the best advantage. Great for them, but not so good for me.

So I decided that sales no longer suited me and spent eighteen months as a self-employed computer installation engineer. For the first year things went very well, and I earned a good living. However then the company began losing contracts, and the work trailed off. I then stumbled on what was, until recently, the happiest time in my working life.

A friend worked for a company that had a contract with the Department for Work and Pensions to provide support and guidance to disabled and unemployed people who wanted to start their own business. With my background, I was ideally suited and was very successful, helping many of my clients to launch their small business and eventually move away from benefits. This was a role where, for the first time in my life, I was making a difference. Helping people and getting paid to do it (not very well as it happens, but that's another story) this ended when they lost the contract, and I was made redundant; the day before my 48th birthday.

A three week stint with my brother convinced me that becoming a plumber was not for me. However a friend of his ran a company supplying electronic security equipment (alarms, CCTV etc.) Spending a couple of days helping him out as a favour led me to successfully apply for a sales role with one of the big national companies in the market.

"I thought you said you'd enough of sales?, I hear you say." Yes, I did. However needs must. I had a family to look after and a mortgage to pay. Seem familiar?

I spent nearly ten years in that industry with three large multi-national corporations, rising to became a regional sales manager and part of teams that negotiated deals worth millions of pounds. However gradually as I got older, the corporate culture began to grind me down. My commitment began to slip and my performance with it. Sales are a young man's game and the pressure to perform ever more intense.

Eventually, I realised I needed to find something that would give me a decent living, without the pressure and hassle. Without the endless rounds of conference calls and e-mail trails; Presentations and meetings about meetings. I needed to get off the ship before I was pushed overboard, without a lifejacket. Having run my own business, I knew all the benefits and potential problems. What I wanted was:

- **Something that was recession proof**

- **Something everybody needed**

- **Something that required a skill not everyone could easily do**

- **Something that was flexible enough for the lifestyle I wanted**

- **Something that required minimum upfront investment**

- **Something that didn't require expensive premises**

- **Something where I would not need to spend time chasing creditors for outstanding monies owed. Even better if they paid before you actually carried out the work**

- **Something with a good cash-flow**

- **Something with minimum costs and a good margin**

Not asking for too much then!

I spent six months investigating various jobs, industries and opportunities. Quite probably the same one's you are looking into now. Then one day, I met an old friend at, you guessed, a funeral. When I asked him what he was up to he replied

"I'm a funeral celebrant."

"A what?" I asked.

The rest, as they say, is history.

Background to Funerals in UK

I have officiated at hundreds of funerals, and I am now respected and well known in the geographical area in which I operate. I have dozens of testimonials from satisfied families and as well as making a living from my work as a celebrant, I have the bonus of knowing I have made a difference. The comments, tips and practical steps outlined in the rest of this book have been learned and honed through experience, not just theory. Many will not be taught to you even on the most expensive training courses.

Just over a hundred years ago, everyone was buried in the UK. The first crematorium was opened in Woking in Surrey in 1878 and is still operating. In 1960 there were 148 crematoria, today there are over 250. The percentage of cremations has risen from 35% in 1960 to 73% in 2010. In the U.S. during the same period the figure has risen from 4% to 40%. Much of this shift is due to a reduction in available land, but some are also because of the additional cost of purchasing a plot and other additional charges such as headstones, etc.

The Funeral Industry

The performance of the funeral industry is largely dependent on the number of deaths in the United Kingdom each year, the average age of the population and the level of household disposable income. Data from the Office for National Statistics suggests that, although the death rate has fallen slightly over the past five years, the proportion of the population aged over 75 grew. In combination with rising household disposable income, this has provided favourable conditions for industry growth.

The UK funeral industry generates around £2bn of revenue. This has increased by around 5% since 2008. There are approximately 1500 business in the industry employing 23,000 people.

According to a recent report, funeral costs continue to rise well above the rate of inflation, and many people are either unaware or unprepared for the costs involved. The report highlights that:

• The average cost of a funeral in the UK is £3284, 6.2 per cent higher than 2011

• The average cost of dying in the UK is £7114 (this is the total average cost assuming all services are used, including discretionary funeral costs such as death and funeral notices, flowers, vehicle and venue hire, memorial)

In October 2012 the Office for National Statistics reported that 484,367 deaths were registered in England and Wales in 2011, 53,661 in Scotland and 14,204 in Northern Ireland. There were around 750,000 births. Mortality rates are falling, and we are all living longer, which is great. However the simple fact that the population is growing and as the famous quote says 'there is nothing certain in this world except......' we will all require the services of a funeral director at some point, sooner or later.

Most people avoid talking about death in what can appear to be an unsympathetic and business-like manner. My experience is that everyone in the industry is committed to providing the highest level of professional care to their clients. However the fact is that people pass away, their remains need to be taken care of and their loved ones wish to say goodbye in a dignified way. Therefore, people will offer these services and over time the industry will emerge. One could argue that the arms industry deals in death as much as the funeral trade.

The term funeral director refers to the company as opposed to an individual. The person whom you see walking in front of a hearse is the funeral conductor. In a small company, the owner may also conduct funerals. In larger groups, they may have a number of individuals who are qualified to perform this role. The funeral advisor or arranger is the person who meets with the family and looks after their specific requirements throughout the process. It is they who have the relationship with the client. This is a crucial factor when it comes to the role of celebrant.

National companies

The funeral market in the UK has two industry leaders, The Co-operative Group (CWS Ltd) and Dignity Caring Funeral Services (Dignity Plc). The Co-operative Group (CWS Ltd) has over 675 branches across the UK and conduct around 90,000 funerals a year. They also own the North Eastern Co-operative. Dignity has just over 500 branches and conducts 75,000 funeral a year. Between these 2 companies, they are currently involved in over 25% of all funerals in the UK.

There are also several privately owned companies who are conducting large numbers of funerals in the UK.

There are several other groups with large numbers of funeral homes. These are different Co-op Groups (mainly regional co-op's) The Midland Co-operative Society, Southern Co-operative Society, United Co-operative Society, Yorkshire Co-operative Society, Lincoln Co-operative Society, Leeds Co-operative Society, Oxford, Swindon & Gloucester Co-operative Society, Heart of England Co-operative Society, Anglia

Regional Co-operative Society, Chelmsford Star Co-operative Society.

Independent regional groups

Larger groups of funeral directors who, whilst resisting the lure of the national players such as Dignity, want the collective strength that being part of a collective gives. The Funeral Services Partnership is one such organisation, although this is spreading its wings nationally.

Independent local groups

These are geographically based companies, normally well established. They have developed a reputation over a sustained period, sometimes over 100 years and can still command a high percentage of the local market. They may have ten or more branches.

Small independents

These are family owned businesses. They may have just a single branch, or perhaps three of four, covering a fairly small geographical area

The role of the celebrant

Over the last twenty years or so the requirement for the non-religious funeral service has gradually grown. This was initially filled by Humanists. Humanists do not believe in God or religion and ceremonies taken by a Humanist, under their strict beliefs, will not allow for ANY religious content whatsoever.

A growing number of families now feel that the church plays little or no part in their lives. Many only attend for christenings, weddings and funerals and have no relationship with a church or the minister. So when it comes to choosing the right person to officiate at a ceremony for their loved one, they feel little or no affinity. Some clergy is reluctant to officiate at a ceremony for those who are not regular church goers, particularly if it is to be held at the crematorium and not the church itself. Of course, there are members of the clergy who give excellent service and will tailor it to the family's needs. However others work under their own terms and can be inflexible.

So the role of the celebrant has evolved and is becoming ever more popular. At present around 30-35% of funerals are conducted by a celebrant. This is growing steadily as their existence becomes more widely known and accepted. Over time the number of people choosing this option will undoubtedly increase as, some would say sadly, the establishment of the church plays a diminishing part if the lives of the majority.

A Celebrant led service will:

• Focus on and be centred on the person who has died, not religion

• Allow relatives and friends a greater contribution to the service and to share their feelings and memories

- Have a warmth and sincerity many bereaved people find lacking in a clergy led service. They are pleased to have provided a ceremony their loved ones would have wanted

- Celebrate the life of the deceased who has died by paying tribute to them, to the life they lived, the people they knew and left behind

- Be more appropriate for those who have not lived according to religious principles, or accepted religious views of life or death

A good celebrant will make sure that the ceremony belongs by the family. It should contain as little or as much religious content as they wish. Even if the funeral advisor tells you the family

"Want a humanist ceremony," approach with an open mind as this will often just mean

"We don't want a full religious ceremony."

Becoming a celebrant can be a rewarding career, both emotionally and financially. It is as far removed from the corporate world many now inhabit and it is as stress free as any modern day role can be. You will be your own boss, in control of your own destiny. That does not mean you can spend half of every day on the golf course or in the garden as some people would have you believe.

However, you will have more flexibility to fit in the things you want and need to do. You will find yourself working harder than you may have done when employed by someone else, but you will have the knowledge that every penny you earn ends up in your pocket. The increasing need for the services a celebrant can provide means the market is growing. The costs of performing the role are simple and relatively low.

- A computer and internet connection

- A decent printer, black and white is fine. Laser is faster and cheaper to run than inkjet

- Paper (low cost is fine for your own needs. 100gsm where you are sending a script to a client)

- An A4 folio and a decent pen (a chewed up biro gives the wrong impression!)

- A reliable car and the normal running costs associated with it

- A decent Sat Nav with traffic warning system

As a self-employed person, you will need the services of an accountant. See the section on running a business for further information.

Fees

These will vary depending on where you live but are around £140-£200. You can establish what the rate is in your area by talking to your local funeral directors. Don't be tempted to reduce your fees as it's extremely unlikely that any advisor will select a celebrant solely based on price. Remember the funeral will cost thousands so decisions on a celebrant, a vital and very visual element, will not be made on the basis of ten or twenty pounds. Unlike flowers, service sheets and other 'disbursements', the funeral directors do not, in most cases, add any amount to what you charge. Check this out to be certain

Some celebrants charge extra for expenses if the service is outside a set distance. You should think very carefully before deciding to levy any such charges as it only serves to create anomalies and confusion in the minds of the funeral advisors. They will have a figure in their minds for the cost of a celebrant and once quoted to the family will be difficult to change. They will be less likely to call you if your pricing is different. This is especially true if their number one choice is unable to take the ceremony and they start to ring around.

Normally the scattering of ashes is offered for a nominal fee or free of charge. This will rarely be carried out on the same day as, once the ceremony is complete, the body may not be cremated and the ashes ready for at least 24 hours. Bear in mind that accepting a separate booking for this could prevent you from taking another fee paying one.

It is also accepted practice within the industry not to charge a fee when officiating at the ceremony for a child under 16. Most funeral directors themselves offer a basic service without charge or only levy a nominal fee for any 'extras'. You are in no way obliged to waive your fee, but it will almost certainly pay off in the amount goodwill it generates. Be a little cautious about taking on such a ceremony early in your career as they are the most heart-breaking and draw of every part of experience.

If you conduct a single service each day of a five day week, then based on a typical fee of £170, you will generate revenue of around £3000 per month. That's an annual income of over £36,000.

Is it for me?

The role of the celebrant is not for everyone. Many people cannot see themselves spending their time surrounded by what they see as grieving people and hearses where everyone dresses in black and has glum faces. If this is your first reaction, then perhaps it is not for you. The fact is that people who work in the industry are just that; people. They like to smile at the appropriate time and enjoy what they do.

You need to have an instinctive empathy with people. If you do not enjoy listening to others, then you will quickly become unsettled when you have to spend an hour listening to someone talk about themselves and their family. You can share some of your own experiences, in many ways this can help create a sense of understanding in the client. However, you must never forget this in not about you.

You will need to be available during the normal working week and on the odd Saturday. Trying to fit the role around a normal 9-5 job is not easy as funeral advisors will expect you to be available when they call. If you keep turning jobs down for whatever reason, they will quickly stop calling. If you are working shifts then you may have more flexibility to be available during the day.

Predicting revenue is almost impossible. You can have a busy period and suddenly find bookings dry up for no apparent reason. Funeral advisors will tell you that they are not busy or that they get periods where clients want a member of the clergy or have requested a named celebrant who has officiated at another funeral in the past. So you must be able to cope with these periods.

Being self-employed means, you will have no sick pay or holidays. Taking time off, particularly in the first year, is tricky as you may have to turn away bookings. During the early days, you will probably be offered work only when the normal first or second choice celebrant is unavailable. Having to turn this down is to be avoided at all costs if you want to reach your target as quickly as possible.

If any of these things ring an alarm bell then think carefully. Any negativity will eventually show itself in your ability to perform the role. It will show in your face and your voice and if the feedback given by the family to the funeral advisor is not good, then your bookings will quickly fall off.

I am not writing this book as an advert for the industry, or to convince you to buy a product or service. Too many of these publications seem to sugar coat everything and some internet sites extol the virtues and ignore the downsides and realities. I set out to write something that gives you the facts and share some of the experiences I have encountered.

On the positive side, being a celebrant can be an enormously rewarding role. Helping a family through a difficult time and making a real contribution to their final goodbye to a loved one can make a real difference. You will receive many heartfelt messages of thanks, something unlikely to happen in most roles, in today's world. Its only people like teachers, doctors and those in social care who share this feeling.

You can make a career if you have the right attributes and are willing to work hard and be patient and determined.

Becoming a Celebrant

Having decided that this is something you wish to do, what next? As the need for celebrant's increases, an industry has grown in providing training and representation. Whilst it would be virtually impossible and very irresponsible to present yourself to funeral directors as a celebrant without proper guidance and knowledge, there is no legal requirement to attend a training course and no pre-qualification conditions.

Training

You can pay anything from £500- £3000 for a training course. What you get for your money varies depending on whether the course is residential and not surprisingly, the number of days. Most offer a certificate and/or membership of a trade body on completion. Those that are more expensive and longer tend to include more information on the aspects surrounding death and also can offer more in depth and comprehensive training on writing, interviewing and presentation skills. There is no single body that represents celebrants such as the Humanist Society, so it is a personal decision as to what benefits are gained from membership.

You should decide what level of training you need to be able to take on the booking from a funeral director. Doing so without the confidence, ability and information needed will result in a very short career. Being a celebrant can be extremely rewarding in many ways, but it is a role with no grey areas or room for error.

Running a business

If you have never run a business or been self-employed before, setting things up can seem a little daunting. Accountants, vat, tax returns, record keeping and the dread of the knock on the door at 3am haunt some people and put them off. If you are genuinely concerned and believe this will keep you awake at night, then perhaps you should think carefully. The reality, however, is nowhere near as frightening. Below are just a few basic points to consider. You should consult an accountant as soon as you can, preferably one who has been used by someone you know.

Informing HMRC

Depending on what route you choose, you will at some point need to inform the HMRC that you are now self-employed or a director. In the case of a sole trader, this must normally be done within 3 months of issuing your first invoice. Limited companies are a little more involved, but any decent accountant will guide you through the process and can even complete the formalities on your behalf. They are not as scary as some people will have you believe. Just take the time to investigate what they need, and you will have no problems. If, in doubt, you can always ring them. The stories of them eating little babies are somewhat exaggerated.

Work will probably start slowly and may take months to reach the target minimum revenue you need. Assuming you have a target of one booking a day this could take up to a year to achieve on a consistent basis. You need to consider carefully how your finances will cope with this. Perhaps you have some savings to give you a buffer or your partner contributes to the household costs. By far the easiest most effective option is to have some other form of income. Look at what things you could do that will bring in some revenue, but still give you the flexibility needed to accept bookings. By planning ahead, you will have a greater chance of reaching your goal without the need to become desperate, a sure fire route to failure.

It's unlikely that you will generate enough revenue working solely as a celebrant, to qualify for compulsory VAT registration. You need to have a turnover (revenue) exceeding £79,000 (2013/14 tax year). If you do exceed this then this will be a wonderful problem to have.

However, your accountant will advise on what strategies are best to tackle this issue.

If your sole or main income source is from celebrant bookings, then you are unlikely to have the amount and type of costs that will make voluntary registration worthwhile. Again your accountant will elaborate.

Limited or sole trader? Your accounting costs will be higher as a limited company, but your potential tax and national insurance liabilities could be lower. As a general rule of thumb (at the time of writing), if you anticipate generating more than £20,000 in profits, then limited liability is probably more efficient.

Your main cost is likely to be your vehicle. There are two ways of claiming back these expenses. Mileage allowance and actual cost. In the first, you simply keep a record of all your business mileage and claim this at the rate of 45p per mile for the first 10,000 and 25p thereafter. No other costs can are allowable and this includes fuel as the rate per mile is calculated to include all your running costs and depreciation. The other method requires you to keep receipts for every item of expenditure such as fuel, oil, road tax, repairs and servicing. In addition, you can claim for the depreciation in the value of the car over a number of years. Set against this, the revenue will assume that you use the car for your own personal use as well as for business purposes. You will have to declare what percentage is business. The revenue is unlikely to accept a figure above 75% if you have a normal car. Your own circumstances will dictate which is best. Assuming you have a computer and printer, you will only need to allow for stationary and printing, a few items of clothing include several black ties (it's doubtful you will be allowed to claim clothing unless you can prove its exclusively for business use) and…….. well that's just about it.

Unless you have complicated financial affairs, it's almost certain that you will require less revenue from your business to produce the net income, you need than working for someone else and paying PAYE.

This is a book about becoming a celebrant and not a guide to tax, etc. so I will not waste any more time on the subject here. There are thousands of books available and millions of pages on the internet.

(You should consult an accountant or other professional and not make decisions based solely on the above information. HMRC rules can and will change so please check)

Choosing a printer

You do not need an expensive printer. If you have one at home then the easiest thing to do is utilise that in the early weeks until the longer term picture becomes clearer. It's sometimes tempting to rush out and buy lots of shiny new toys when starting a new business. You should avoid that temptation unless you have the funds spare. Better to use the cash as a buffer, particularly if this is to be your sole income source.

Most people are familiar with the cost and quality comparisons between laser and inkjet. I bought an inexpensive laser which cost around £80. It had the advantage of automatic double sided printing which speeds up the time to print and reduces paper usage By searching the internet I was able to buy toner cartridges for around £20. This is the most cost effective and efficient method. Whatever you decide, ensure you have spares available. You do not want to find yourself in the position of running out of ink when you wish to print out a script for a live ceremony.

Revenue projections

A large percentage of bookings will be given to you around 10 days prior to the service, as this is the time when the funeral advisor has booked everything else and is now looking to secure a person to officiate. This means that you should know what bookings you have in good time to plan ahead.

Whilst funerals have, of course a fixed time and date, family visits allow you greater flexibility to carry out other work.

Cash-flow

Another popular business saying is that turnover is vanity; profit is sanity. What they forgot to add was that cash-flow is reality.

One of the main reasons that businesses' fail, whether new or established, is because they run out of cash. There are countless examples of profitable companies with full order books that have ceased trading because they did not have enough money in the bank to meet their liabilities.

Most people, whether large corporations or sole traders will, unless dealing directly with the public, have to invoice their customer and then wait until the money to be paid. Normal practice is to allow creditors at least 30 days before they are required to settle. Given that few companies pay on time without at least one reminder call, this often stretches to 45 days or even 60. In some industries, it can take even longer. Talk to someone working as a contractor in the construction industry.

In some of the industries that you may be considering a new career, the company will have a policy of retentions. This can include sales of some home improvement products. This is where an employer will keep back a percentage of the payment due to you in case of problems arise which are due to poor performance on that part of the employee or agent. This could be straightforward miss-selling or a mistake in, for example, measuring room dimensions, which lead to issues. This sounds fair as it helps prevent cowboys from taking advantage. However, there are many stories of unscrupulous company's deliberately and unfairly withholding monies for months, or simply not paying at all.

Unfortunately, those to whom you owe money and incredibly this could even be the same company you are chasing, will be asking you to pay them as soon as possible. This movement of money, in and out of the business is known as cash-flow. If at any point in time, the flow of money out is not matched or exceeded by that coming in, you will have a problem. Many companies have to rely on an overdraft facility to bridge this gap. However, these are expensive and put your fate in the hands of those kind hearted and philanthropic people at your local bank.

One of the great things about working as a celebrant is the fact that you will be paid by cheque or BACS either before the ceremony or on the day. This is an accepted practice with every funeral director. You can probably quote another business where they receive money before the goods are handed over. The retail trade is one and others such as tradesmen and women. The difference with being a celebrant is that, unlike these others, you have no stock to buy beforehand.

The business model of a celebrant is as near perfect as you can get. Positive cash-flow, no stock, extremely low overheads (costs to run the business). Depending on the industry, the company will be looking to make a margin (the difference between what it earns and spends) of around 35%. Supermarkets, for instance, work on well under 10%. Assuming you can get to the point where you are carrying out 3 or 4 funerals a week, the margins of a celebrant are nearer 80%.

Starting Out

Initial fact-finding

Decide how far you are prepared to travel from home. Get a hold of a map and draw a rough circle taking into account motorways, etc. Make a note of all the towns inside this area and type these onto a spreadsheet. Make a separate tab for each county, town, etc. depending on its size, then take to the internet. Type in "funeral directors in xxx" into a search engine and it will give you a list of branches. Some will be nationals, some independents.

Make a note of these and capture the following:

- Name

- Group (if any)

- Address

- Telephone

- Any contact names

Visiting local funeral directors

Once you have your list of the funeral directors that are located within your chosen target area, you should plan to visit them. Make sure you dress smartly, but there is no need for a black tie.

If you are on a fact finding mission to test the market for celebrants, a couple in each town will give you the information you need. Some questions you could ask include:

- Do you use celebrants?

- What % of your services are currently

  led by a celebrant?

- Whom do you use at present?

- What is the normal fee charged?

This will enable you to gauge the size of the market, the competition and your potential revenue. Don't be put off if you get a lukewarm reception. Most funeral directors will be using a few celebrants. However, most will want to have a pool from which to choose. Initially, this will be when the first and second choices are busy or away.

How do I get my first booking?

This is seen as the biggest stumbling block to making a successful career. There is no magic answer. The important thing is to work at creating a degree of trust with the advisor. Remember when they recommend you, they are putting both their own and their company's reputation at risk. If you do not give the level of service they expect, the family will not just blame you. All the hard work and attention to detail they (and you) put in will all be forgotten because the celebrant forgot to read out the poem that was chosen!

Marketing

Being a celebrant is not a career where masses of advertising and smart marketing will lead to growth in your business. You could spend a fortune on glossy brochures, very impressive interactive website, sophisticated internet ad campaign that gets you at the top whenever someone types in celebrant, in your area. However would you see a return on your investment?

The vast majority of families will use the celebrant recommend by their funeral advisor. Some will have seen one at another ceremony or heard through a friend or relative.

So your efforts must be targeted on those who will provide you with the vast majority of your work.

Web site

It is a good idea to have a web site as many people see it as a weakness if you do not have one. However, there is no need to spend a fortune on it. There are several companies including VistaPrint and 1-1 who will allow you to create something simple and only charge a few pounds a month to host the site. If this is not something you can do yourself, there are plenty of people who can.

However again, be careful about spending large sums, particularly in the early days. You can easily find yourself drawn into the world of the techies who will soon have you believing you simply MUST have a site to rival the BBC. Check out the sites of other celebrants, and you will find that most are simple. It just needs to have basic information on you and what you do. Once you have a few testimonials, it's a good idea to put these up, as well. You may wish to add additional information such as poems, readings, etc. over time. Be careful not to spend too much time on the computer and NEVER at the expense of getting out in front of your potential clients.

Pamphlets

Again no need for a 24 page booklet. For around £40-£50, you can get 250 double sided full colour pamphlets. With the correct wording, these can be given to both funeral directors and families. Better still the funeral advisor can show the family. This is ok in the early days.

Business cards

If you shop around you can get some great deals on business cards. However don't be tempted to go for the freebie ones. Everyone knows these and they often have the website printed on the back. They shout "I'm doing this on the cheap." Pay a little extra and go for the premium version on a decent card stock. These cards are not for clients, but funeral directors.

E-mail

EMAILS-mails are not a good way to initially market yourself as they can be seen as impersonal and give the recipient no idea of your personality or how you come across. You need to get face time. Once established, they can be used to stay in touch, but not at this stage.

Shoe leather

There is no substitute for getting in the car and pounding the streets. It's amazing how much information you will pick up this way. To save your expensive fuel, work out which locations you wish to visit and armed with their postcodes head for Google maps or something equivalent and plan a circular route.

Building the number of funerals

Your first booking will be both an exciting and nerve-wracking experience. Make sure you actively seek feedback from the advisor. It's probably best not to contact the family after the ceremony as they are still coping with their grief. If you are good at what you do, you will soon start to receive thank you messages.

It can take quite a while to build things up, so don't despair. In the early days, it's just important to be available and to return any calls promptly. Advisors hate celebrants that delay or even fail to reply to a message. It's ok to leave your answer phone activated as most will be happy to leave a message.

100% right 100% of the time

Most funeral directors have a choice of celebrants. Your goal is to become one of their top choices, so they call you first, or second. If they do not then your details will probably be in a) the bottom of a drawer b) a file c) a computer list of approved suppliers. This will often depend on whether the branch is a single site, part of a small independent group, part of a group under a larger umbrella or part of a national company such as the Co-op or Dignity. You must create a process to ensure you do not make any of the obvious mistakes..

Meeting the Family

Once you have received the notification from the funeral director, you should contact the family member as directed by them. This contact may not necessarily be the person whom the funeral director regard as the chief mourner, the person who has contracted with them to carry out the funeral. It's important to establish who the chief mourner is because, in the event of any conflicting instructions, it is he or she who will have the final say.

Control within the meeting

The family interview is usually with close members of the family. Be ready for as many as six or more to be present including children and for some of them to come and go. If the interview is not with the close family but someone representing them, it is important to establish that the wishes of the close family are being followed.

Meeting people on your own

In today's world, this element should not be ignored. Make sure the person knows you are happy to have a friend/relative/neighbour in attendance. When making the appointment, some people ask where the meeting will be held. Let them know you are happy to meet anywhere they wish, even in a public place if that's what they want. You may wish to consider obtaining a CRB certificate for the added peace of mind of your clients.

Welcoming

Ensure your clothing is as you want it to be before you get to the door. Are your shoes clean? Your collar tucked in? Your tie straight? You're dress as you want it? Remember the old adage that people make decisions about us in the first 30 seconds? Well, it's true in so far as this initial impression is one that is very difficult and takes a long time to change.

Introduce yourself and offer a handshake. Remember this is not a business meeting so there is no need to think you must give a firm grip. Be led by the other person. Give a warm, but not too over enthusiastic smile. Offer handshakes to everyone you meet as you enter. If someone new comes in, and you are seated, always stand.

Starting off

Your initial welcome to the family needs to convey your understanding of their situation. You need to ensure they are comfortable with you and will, therefore, open up to you. Above all, they need to feel confident that they have made the right decision in having a civil funeral and be assured that you will take care of the ceremony for them and their loved one.

Style

Be relaxed. Explain:

- The role of the celebrant

- How you differ from a religious minister at one end and a Humanist at the other.

- That it is the family's ceremony, not yours. You are there to help, guide and work with the family and the funeral director to ensure that every aspect of the ceremony is exactly as they envisaged and reflects the deceased's personality and wishes.

Don't use the wrong name

If unsure write it on your pad (that goes for relatives too). This is one of the quickest routes to putting the family on the defensive and causing issues further down the line. It's not uncommon for a family to ask the funeral director for another celebrant when someone has made this mistake more than once during the meeting.

You need to be careful not to show any surprise or adverse reaction whatever you may be told. If you do, it may prevent the family revealing any more information. You need to be gentle and probing and appear genuinely interested in what you are hearing. The process of talking to you can be quite calming, and they will surprise themselves by how much information that they will provide you. Even in the most difficult of situations.

Questioning techniques

Open Questions- How? What? Where? When? Why?

Targeted Questions- What exactly? How much?

Searching- Was that a happy moment? Could you explain that a little more?

Delving deeper- And then what happened next?

Remember to be yourself. All the techniques and tips should be used to develop and stamp your own personality and style to the role. You will not be able to keep up a totally false persona over months and hopefully years, so don't try. The role of celebrant is not for everyone, and the ability to maintain a professional distance is paramount.

Listening techniques

Sales trainers say that you should talk and listen in the same proportion as the organs we use for the tasks i.e. two ears and one mouth.

Listening is what enables us to understand and gather the vital information we need to create a ceremony that reflects and captures who the person was. Listening means clearing your mind and doing more than just hearing the words. The tone, inflection and passion with which they are delivered help us to understand the speaker's feelings and decide what's important and, therefore, what we need to emphasise.

Listening also creates empathy, the feeling in the client that you are interested in what they have to say. That leads to a greater depth in what they will tell you.

Remember 80% of communication is nonverbal. So we must use our body. to

• Maintain eye contact

• Use your face to express surprise, sorrow, sadness, happiness

• React when someone says something that's obviously heartfelt for them

• Nod and drop in positive word such as "I see," "Oh Yes," "really?"

If you master these techniques naturally you will find the meeting much easier, and you will see the families visibly relax over the time. They will express relief as you leave that they are happy the ceremony is in safe hands.

Explaining the ceremony

It's a good idea to give an outline of the funeral you usually conduct. A typical structure is as follows:

1. Entrance music

2. Opening Words

3. Hymn

4. Poem or reading

5. Tribute

6. Reflection

7. Committal

8. Prayer

9. Closing words

Every situation is different. You could be dealing with a confused partner who is unable to decide on anything or a large family where several members have organised everything down to the last detail.

All these options should be presented to the client as genuine choices, and not you making assumptions. The client may prefer to leave the decisions to you, but everyone concerned need to be clear about this.

Obtaining Information about the deceased

This is an essential skill you must develop. It is not simply a question and answer session. You must make everyone feel as comfortable as possible talking to someone who is, essentially, a stranger in a short period. It's a good idea to have a sheet of some description with all the things you need to know, so you do not forget and have to keep contacting the family. It looks unprofessional and is an easy way to start losing trust. Start with open questions (who, what, why, where, when) that prompt the person to answer in a little detail. Close questions (do you want the curtains closed?) are designed to be answered yes or no. They have their place but not in the early stages of your visit.

Different people see things differently

Generations of the family may like to express their own views, but sometimes their wording may need some attention; many fathers can be thought of by children in terms the widowed mother may not endorse, and vice versa.

You will receive vastly different amounts of information. Often the people who have lived the longest are those whose families know least about them. Many older people do not talk about their early life, particularly if it was difficult. Many war veterans probably won't have said too much to their family's. Many very elderly people have lost most of their peers and so information can be sparse. Just obtain what you can.

Sensitivity and appropriateness

Apart from what is said about the family interview above, the following points are worth noting:

• Be professional and strike a balance between seeming cold and unconcerned at one end and over emotional at the other

• Don't be tempted to try and overstep the mark. You are there to offer a professional service. You almost certainly did not know the deceased or the family. Trying to seem over sincere is likely to make the family feel uncomfortable

• Your aim is to capture and reflect who the deceased was, not give the impression that you are a lifelong family friend.

Families that wish to take an active part in the funeral will need to know about the time constraints within which the funeral must fit.

Selection of readings & poems

Many people expect a funeral to move them in some degree, and the readings need choosing accordingly. Most celebrants develop a selection of poems that they become familiar with and find both helpful and relevant. Suggest those that you feel appropriate to clients, never forgetting that the choice is theirs. Try not to offer too much choice. There are hundreds available on the internet if they are inclined to search. Sending a selection to them may also prove helpful.

Friends and relatives

Situations vary from a family member or friend wishing to read out a poem, through wanting to talk about what the deceased meant to them, to some who will write their own tribute and turn the celebrant's role into more of a master of ceremonies. It's imperative that you stay in control, even when you are faced with a domineering character who is arranging things.

• Point out how long people take to speak.

• Suggest a time limit

• Tell the family member organising things that you need to have everything to hand to ensure the timing fits within the slot

Hymns and prayers

If the family decides to include a hymn, suggest that they have one that people know — otherwise no-one sings! It may be preferable to listen to a recording of a hymn rather than ask the mourners to stand and sing in the usual way.

Do be aware that some hymns are known by their refrain or title, for example, 'Jerusalem' is also known as 'As did those feet' which is the first line. Also ensure that the number and content of the verses matches a) what will be played b) what will be printed in any service sheets.

Should you sing along with the congregation? Firstly you need to know how your voice sounds. This will be a good indicator whether you will help or hinder. However, I think it gives a positive impression if you are seen to be joining in, even at a very low volume.

Music

A source of worries, issues and problems for the family, you and the funeral directors. Make sure you capture the exact title and artist of the choice. If it is a requirement for the family to provide their own music, then the easiest method is for them to supply original CD's for each piece. Advise them to write out the track number and title on a slip of paper that is inserted in the box for each CD and to give them to the funeral director. Let the funeral advisor know this, and you can then rest easy.

If you are dealing with a family who is confused, don't have the CD or any other combination, this is where you need to use your discretion. If there are younger family members who volunteer to acquire the music that becomes a reasonable option. Advise them as above. If they are going to burn a CD then tell them they must get this to the crematorium, either directly or via the funeral director, in good time for them to check it will work on their system.

Music to enter

Playing music while the congregation gathers in the chapel can be helpful in setting the mood, depending upon the number of people, work out how long a piece you will need for the coffin to be brought in, placed on the catafalque and for the conductor and bearers to leave. This will be between three and five minutes. However it's possible to have the music repeated if a particular choice is either short or something happens that causes a delay after it has started. As with everything plan for the unexpected and you will have a contingency to keep things running smoothly.

Music at reflection/committal

The reflection allows the congregation to sit and think about the deceased. The music should, ideally, evoke memories of the person. Requests will be wide-ranging.

Music for exit

Many people like to have something a little upbeat at this point, others something poignant. Favourites include Always look on the bright side of life by Monty Python, My Way by Frank Sinatra We'll meet again by Vera Lynn and Time to say goodbye by Andrea Boccelli.

Music suitability

With such a diverse range of music available now, it's almost impossible to decide what is appropriate. Remember it's the family's ceremony, so don't try to lecture them on what they should choose. I have heard some advice that the entrance music should have a certain beat. My experience is that the bearers carrying the coffin from the hearse will adjust their step to whatever is playing and maintain a dignified pace. That's their job, and they are used to it.

Leaving

Conclude the meeting by asking if there are any points that they wish to discuss, that have not been covered. Ask if everyone is happy with how the meeting has gone (particular attention should be paid to the chief mourner). Remember the 80% rule and pay attention as what they say may not fully reveal what they are thinking.

Writing the script and tribute

The overall aim is to capture the 'essence' of the person and paint a picture with words that reflect who they were.

The words you use at the opening and closing of the ceremony and other times such as the committal should be given to you by your training provider. There should be a selection for each element, enabling you to build a ceremony that you believe is just right.

The tribute has to be written from scratch each time. There is no easy way to teach this. It's a skill you will need to develop. This is when you discover how good you are at taking notes!

Don't try to be clever and show off how good you are. Never forget that you are there to represent the family.

You should be aiming to capture the following type of information. This is not exhaustive and will not be applicable to everyone.

- Date and place of birth

- Parents names

- Sibling names (if any have passed away, you may wish to make a reference to this)

- Where were they brought up?

- Where did they go to school?

- Did they enjoy school- were they a rascal or a scholar?

- Any schoolday anecdotes?

- What did they do on leaving education?

- Rest of career (This may be gleaned all at once or in sections)

- Where and when did they meet their partner? (if appropriate)

- When did they marry and where did they set up home?

- Details of children, grandchildren and great-grandchildren (Let the family decide in what order to give any names. (Name all or none and suggest just giving a number if above 5 or 6 unless specifically told otherwise.)

• Memories of family holidays?

• Hobbies and interests (These could vary for an older person between youth and later years)

• Discuss gently the deceased final days to possibly include a line or two about this.

The congregation may have known the deceased in different situations such as work or a hobby or perhaps a residential home. It's, therefore, important to include all aspects. Your ability to achieve this is dependent on how much information you gather during the family meeting. If a hobby such as golf, is mentioned, ask if anyone from the club will attend and suggest mentioning the club. This will make those attending feel part of the ceremony and increase the feeling amongst everyone that the tribute accurately reflected the deceased's life and interests.

Accuracy is critical. Any errors, however small, will be picked up by someone and quite possibly mentioned afterwards. All your good work could disappear in a single word and all that person will remember is the error. Check and recheck if you are in any way unsure.

What to leave out
• Too much detail of the circumstances surrounding the death of the deceased, unless specifically requested by the family

• Family problems

- Your own poetry

- Where the death was by suicide or the deceased was murdered

- Overuse of the word death. There are alternatives such as passing.

- Apologies

- How you are feeling

Construction

Try to vary the length of sentences to add variety. Short sentences followed by a pause have a great impact if not used too often.

You may wish to set out the script in a way that helps you pause and add emphasis. You will develop your own style and content over time.

Length

For most funerals, the length of the tribute should be about 4-8 minutes. Assume you will speak at around 150 words per minute so you can predict the length. Practicing a tribute several times and timing it, will allow you to gauge your own rate of speech. Family and friends tend to talk a little faster. If a tribute is to be either written or delivered by a family member or friend, ensure you have sight of it as soon as possible.

Humour

There is a place for some element of humour in most tributes. Humour is normally injected by references to things the deceased said or did that were typical of them. Quoting their humour is a good way of reflecting who they were. Again the mood and tone of the family meeting should give you a good indication of what is appropriate. Asking

Names

Use the full name of the deceased at least once, perhaps at the start of the tribute. Check with the family as to what name they wish you to use throughout ensures they are happy. If there is more than one name, then ask the family to decide which they prefer and make reference to the other(s) once at some point in your script.

Officiating at the ceremony

80% of communication is achieved through non-verbal means, so it's vitally important that, from the moment you leave your car, you convey the correct message to everyone around you. This includes the funeral director, their staff and the crematorium personnel.

The fact that you may have given work based presentations to hundreds of people in the past does not automatically qualify you as a good celebrant. The delivery is totally different as is the occasion and your audience. A good celebrant will be able to reach out to the congregation with the pace, tone and inflection of his or her words. It is, in many ways, a performance. One which is designed to convey the essence of the person to the family and the rest of those present. Your words must leave the page and connect on an emotional level.

You should aim for a quiet, calm and respectful aura. Check the details on the daily sheet outside to be 100% sure you have the correct venue and time. Seek out the attendant and check the music. Discuss any particular requirements.

If it's an unfamiliar chapel, make sure you know where the various controls are (these may include closing curtains, signalling the end of the service etc.) and how they function. How are you going to communicate with the attendant? If they use CCTV, where is the camera? Check out the monitor if possible so you know what he/she can see.

If there is an order of service, obtain one and check the content and running order against your script. If there is even the slightest doubt in your mind, discretely check with the family or the funeral conductor when they arrive. Any embarrassment you may feel at asking and any irritation the family may convey, will pale into insignificance when compared to the firestorm that will engulf you make an error.

If you forget an element of a work presentation, then there is always the option to be reminded by a colleague or even to backtrack a few slides. No such luxury exists in your role as a celebrant. Think of it as a rollercoaster ride. Once it has started there is no getting off!

Posture and stance

• Stand upright and avoid moving too much as this will convey a sense of unease

• Stand firmly with feet slightly apart and one foot a few inches in front of the other. Avoid shuffling, which can be distracting.

• Moderate your breathing

• It is not necessary to stay rooted to the spot, but movements should be definite and for a purpose. Avoid too much arm waving as it can be distracting.

• Other distracting actions can include, scratching, fiddling with jewellery, pen or paper, jingling coins, etc.

Contact with the congregation

Once the ceremony begins, it's best to avoid too much direct eye contact with members of the congregation as it can be unnerving for them and distracting for you. It is through our eyes and facial expression that we convey our mood whether it is one of enthusiasm, excitement or boredom. It may be tempting to engage with someone with whom you make eye contact. Focus on a point just above their heads and remember, if the chapel becomes crowded, vary your point of focus so as to include everyone.

Reading for ceremonies

If you have time, try to read through any poetry beforehand and speak it aloud. You may even wish to mark on your script where you want to emphasise a word.

There is a knack to reading prose and only practice will improve your skills in this area

Where others are contributing a reading, you should encourage them to practice at least once. Let them know a little about techniques for pausing and looking up from the script now and again

Verbal skills

Do you know how your voice comes across to the audience?

Most people have not heard themselves speak. It's a good idea to record yourself reading some actual words from a script. You may be surprised at the way you sound to others and how you intonate certain words. Many of us do not fully pronounce our words and whilst that may be ok in conversation, it's not in the role of the celebrant. Heart can easily become 'art and with a soft sound not the required hard t sound.

You may also be tempted to speak a little too fast, particularly when you are inexperienced. When giving a presentation, which is essentially what you are doing, this should be slower than normal conversation. Use the word count feature on your word processor to select 150 words and practice these out loud whilst timing yourself, until you can deliver them within this range. Then record yourself again, or get someone to listen to you. You might think it will sound as if you're speaking in slow motion. However it will not seem that way to your audience.

Some people speak too softly. If you do not project your voice, your message is lost on the congregation. Ask someone if you can are audible at the back of a large room. It's not about shouting or raising your voice. Make sure you learn how to control your breathing, so you do not run out of breath towards the end of an important sentence. Understanding your script helps as it will enable you to make sure you have enough air. Like singing, speaking to an audience requires that the volume comes from your stomach area and not just your throat. If you master this it also helps prevent a dry throat. Practise makes perfect. Most chapels have a sound system with a microphone attached to the lectern, but beware as these also amplify any mistakes!

Variation
If you have ever wondered why some people sound interesting when speaking and other have you reaching for the matchsticks to prop open your eyelids?

If you speak at the same pace and tone you could be announcing the lottery numbers and people would soon lose interest. Listen to prominent people and those on television and take note of how they seem to naturally vary these things. You can use pace, tone and volume to emphasise different emotions such sadness, excitement, humour. For example, why would you put an exclamation mark at the end of a sentence? How are you going to convey the meaning to your audience?

The pace will depend on you. If there has been a lull in the ceremony, it is up to you to pick up the pace again.

Different situations

Coping with your own emotions

You need to be able to lead a funeral with feeling but without your emotions getting out of control. Make sure the script is laid out in a way you can easily read. A minimum of 14pt is advised

•   Practise out loud when you are still inexperienced or at a particularly stressful situation

•   Imagine that the ceremony is for someone else for whom you have previously conducted a funeral

•   If necessary, pause. Take a deep breath and hold it, and then breathe out slowly

- If you still break down, remember you are only human

Emotion in the congregation

It is quite usual for close relations to cry at funerals, especially at the committal or farewell. The celebrant should not draw attention to it. Very rarely, the next-of-kin will break down altogether. Just carry on and avoid eye contact with anyone. If guests become unduly emotional, fellow members of the congregation will comfort them. Don't get involved or stop the ceremony as your focus needs to be on the main family members, and you need to keep things moving.

Speakers unable to continue

If someone reading a poem or the tribute breaks down, give them time to compose themselves — do not automatically take over. If you believe someone looks extra tense when you have seen the family, suggest they get someone to join them. This gives a great sense of comfort. In extreme cases and only with their consent, take over.

Numbers

Generally the older a person is, the fewer will attend, but with a death before retirement age, the numbers will usually be greater than the family expects. Where a death occurs before the mid 20's, the numbers may be very large. This also applies if the diseased was a member of a club or association.

Your interest in numbers is to allow you to factor in the correct amount of time for the congregation to enter and exit the chapel. Anything less than 50 will normally take no longer 3-4 minutes. On the odd occasion, people remain inside chatting, particularly if the curtains have remained open.

Things going wrong & other situations

As with anything in life, mistakes and accidents can happen. As a celebrant, you cannot afford any that are attributable to you as it will have an immediate and negative effect on your reputation and bookings. Sometimes even things that are not your direct responsibility may be seen as such and have a similar effect.

Anything that can go wrong will, so you must prepare for all contingencies. You will hear many stories of ministers reading the wrong script, getting people's names wrong and countless other mistakes. Another common mistake is turning up with a version of the script that doesn't include the last set of changes sent by the client or failing to invite a family member or friend to deliver their eulogy or poem.

You will become all too aware of how important these things are if you ever get that awful feeling when, part way through the ceremony, you realise you have made a mistake.

Joint funerals

It is possible to hold a ceremony for more than one person. The following are the main points to consider:

- The ceremony will usually need to be at least twice the usual length.

- Both families need to agree on the content

- Ensure equal time is given to each family

In these circumstances, it's possible the numbers attending may exceed the limit of the chapel. Some sites where they have several chapels will allow the proceedings to be delayed. It is possible to have an infant placed in the same coffin as the parent if they died together. Don't be tempted to demand a double fee as one celebrant I know of did. The ceremony did not last any longer than that for one person and the family were not very pleased. Needless to say, neither were the funeral directors. The same goes for double slots. These will normally last an hour and are suggested where there is a very large congregation (150+) or the family have a large number of speakers.

Burials

A burial service led by a celebrant will differ only in the obviously different committal of the deceased's body. A member of the clergy will always lead a burial in a consecrated churchyard, so this situation will rarely, if ever, arise.

However municipal cemeteries and areas within the grounds of a crematorium have no such limitations. Whether in the crematorium or a chapel within a cemetery, the coffin will be placed on two trestles throughout the ceremony and moved to the graveside by hearse. It's a good idea to keep the words you use to a minimum at this point. The majority of the ceremony should be conducted in the chapel as it is a better environment and not at risk from the elements. The internment of the coffin only takes half a minute, and your words should reflect this.

Graveside Ceremony

Occasionally you may be asked to conduct a graveside ceremony if no chapel exists at the cemetery. If a family does not wish to have a ceremony at another venue i.e. a crematorium, then in all probability they will want something fairly short. Unless a portable CD player is provided, music is an issue. The congregation will be gathered around the grave, and your voice will soon get lost in the wind and elements. As always, discuss what the family want, but suggest limiting the ceremony to 10- 15 minutes

Other venues

As people move away from religion, a trend that has created the role of funeral celebrant, the venue at which funerals take place is also changing. This can include scattering of ashes in a particular spot that had special meaning to the family. A number of woodland burial sites have also opened in the last few years which offer a complete alternative to the chapel based venues. One I have worked at conveys the coffin from the pavilion to the graveside in a horse and cart, offering lifts for the return journey. The whole atmosphere is different, and your ceremony should reflect this. It does not necessarily mean that the family is anti-religious, so approach your information gathering with an open mind.

What Next?

I make my living working as a celebrant. I am also an author, and I have combined the two in producing this book. I was prompted by a telephone call I received a few months ago from a man whose wife had attended a particularly challenging funeral I had lead. He was considering training to become a celebrant and was keen to talk.

After half an hour, he asked me whether I would consider training him. He said that he believed learning on the job from a working celebrant would be more effective than anything he could learn in the classroom. So I agreed and developed a 3 day 1-1 course. It was a great success, and he is now starting his career.

I will consider repeating this course for anyone residing outside of my working 'patch.' I am confident that anyone I train will have all the tools necessary to build a successful career and will offer ongoing support. As I make my living from doing the job and not just training others, I would be creating my own competition and lose some of the 'edge' I have established if I were to offer this to someone operating in proximity to me.

If you are interested, send me an e-mail giving some information on your background, the relevant skills you have and where you live. I will send you more information and course content. There are also a few additional practicable tips that I will share with you.

Whatever you decide to do, I hope you have found this book useful, even if you decide that the role is not for you. The price of this book will definitely be less than any training course. You must be able to empathise with people. Attention to detail and business skills are also as important as your local funeral directors will have a growing pool of people offering their services. You need to be able to make an instant impression and stand out from the crowd. I can show you how. Because that's what I did.

Good Luck

John P Ford

john.ford@outlook.com

All figures are correct at the time of writing (April 2014). You should always seek advice from a professional before committing to any course of action involving a financial commitment. Whilst the information in this book is given in good faith and is accurate to the best of the author's knowledge, it should be independently verified and not used solely to make any decisions, financial or otherwise.

Glossary

Arrangement Room

A room at the where the family can discuss the necessary arrangements with the advisor.

Bereaved

The family of the deceased.

Burial

Underground committal of a body

Burial Certificate

Legal papers required to enable a cremation or burial to take place.

Casket

A receptacle in which the body is placed for cremation or burial. Commonly called a coffin.

Catafalque

A platform where the coffin is placed for the duration of the cremation ceremony.

Cemetery

A piece of land set aside for the burial of remains.

Ceremony

A gathering of family and friends at a place set aside for such a purpose. A non-religious funeral is generally referred to in this manner.

Chief Mourner

The person who is designated by the funeral director as the individual with whom they are contracted and whose wishes are regarded as final.

Committal

Moment at a burial when the coffin is lowered into the ground. At a cremation this is substituted for closing of the curtains.

Cremation

The process by which the body is reduced to ashes.

Disbursements

Charges levied by a funeral director for additional services such as flowers, service sheets and the officiate.

Embalming

Preserving the body by injecting a fluid into the veins.

Eulogy

A speech that celebrates the life and achievements of the deceased.

Funeral Advisor

An individual who deals directly with family members and arranges the various elements such as flowers, booking the venue, arranging the officiate and being a point of contact for all queries.

Funeral Director

A term used to describe an individual who is qualified to prepare a body for a funeral and lead the event on the day. It is also used to describe a company who offers these services.

Internment

To place ashes into an urn. The process of creating the ashes that most people would recognise has two stages. The remains that are removed from the cremator contain many large pieces of bone and any metal objects such as replacement hips etc. These must be separated and the bones reduced to a powder like substance.

Officiate

A person who conducts the funeral ceremony. This could be a religious minister, a humanist or a celebrant. There is no requirement to have such a person attend any funeral or cremation.

Pallbearers

Employees of the funeral director or family members who transport the coffin from the hearse to the chapel.

Reposing Room

A room at a funeral director's premises where the body is stored prior to the funeral.

Service

Similar to a ceremony, but used mainly when describing a religious based funeral.

Wake

An Irish term for the reception held after a funeral.

6435745R00045

Printed in Great Britain
by Amazon.co.uk, Ltd.,
Marston Gate.